HAPPY FEET

The Savoy Ballroom Lindy Hoppers and Me

RICHARD MICHELSON

ILLUSTRATED BY E. B. LEWIS

GULLIVER BOOKS · HARCOURT, INC.

ando AUSTIN NEW YORK
iego TORONTO LONDON

www.HarcourtBooks.com

Gulliver Books is a trademark of Harcourt, Inc., registered in
the United States of America and/or other jurisdictions.

Library of Congress Cataloging-in-Publication Data
Michelson, Richard.
Happy feet: the Savoy Ballroom Lindy Hoppers and me/by Richard Michelson;
illustrated by E. B. Lewis.
p.   cm.
Summary: A young boy who loves to dance listens as his father retells
the story of the night he was born, which coincided with the opening
of the Savoy Ballroom in Harlem.
[1. Dance—Fiction.   2. Fathers and sons—Fiction.   3. African Americans—Fiction.
4. Harlem (New York, N.Y.)—History—20th century—Fiction.]
I. Lewis, Earl B., ill.   II. Title.
PZ7.M581915Hap   2005
[Fic]—dc22   2004024399
ISBN 0-15-205057-4

C E G H F D B

Printed in Singapore

The illustrations in this book were done in watercolor on Arches paper.
The display type was set in OPTIMargueritte.
The text type was set in OPTIFlorentine.
Color separations by Bright Arts Ltd., Hong Kong
Printed and bound by Tien Wah Press, Singapore
This book was printed on totally chlorine-free
104 gsm Cougar Opaque Natural Woodfree paper.
Production supervision by Pascha Gerlinger
Designed by Kristine Brogno and Scott Piehl

For the Forrestos:
Merm, Shek, Stu and Zuk.
Still the Coolest Cats
—R. M.

To Mr. Fuller at Fuller Shoeshine.
Thanks for everything
—E. B. L.

I'm sittin' in Pop's
Shoeshine Shop.
My toes are tappin',
and my knees are swingin'.

My daddy calls me
Happy Feet
because I was born on
a special day.

Mama says any day I was born would be special,
but Daddy says the twelfth of March 1926
was extra special.

It was the day the doors swung open on the earth's
hottest, coolest,
most magnificent,
superdeluxe dancing palace.

The Savoy!

Outside our window the line's
already snakin' down Lenox.
I wave to Stretch and Shorty.
"Maybe today I'll see
Musclehead," I say.

The bell jangles and Whitey walks in.
He's muggin' as he gives me some skin.
All the hep cats come to Pop's.

My daddy was smart. He knew the Savoy
would bring thousands of feet beatin' down
this street, so he worked hard to help build it.

He banged nails.
He mopped floors.
He hauled boxes.

Some days Daddy didn't even stop for dinner.
His dream was to open his own shop,
and he saved every dime he made.

Then, on the night I was born, he set his hand-painted sign in his very own shop's window:

* *

**STEP UP FOR
THE FINEST SHINE
IN HARLEM**

*

**SEE THE MOON *SWIMMING*
IN YOUR SHOES**

* *

Long-Legged George gets up
from his stool and pays me
before he picks up his coat.
"Ask your daddy about
the night he outdanced
Twistmouth George,"
he jives.

I drop the deuce
in the cash register.
"That's my favorite
story," I say.
Daddy's eyes light up.
It's his favorite, too.

"On the night you were born," my daddy tells me,
"all of Harlem togged out in their finest threads,
leaving their hard, working lives behind.
Even the rich white dukes came flying in from
Hollywood, driving down in their limousines."

"When folk are swinging," Whitey sings, "ain't nobody better than nobody!

Salt and pepper—equals! Cats and chicks—equals! Everybody just coming to dance."

"Your mama was upstairs, resting,"
my daddy says,
"with a dancing baby
in her belly."
I smile because I know
Daddy's spoutin'
about me.

Daddy smiles, too.

"I was locking up," he tells me,
"and listening hard for your mama,
when Twistmouth himself
knocked on the door,
asking the cost of a premium shine.
'No charge,' I told him, 'it's jelly on the cuff.'

'Well then, alligator,' he said,
'are your boots laced?'
And he ticketed us both across
the street to the head of the line."

"There were ballrooms before,"
my daddy says, "but none like the Savoy.

When we walked in, Big Bea was
sparking a dance so new
it didn't even have a name yet;

Shorty was spinning till he was dizzy;

and Stretch was reinventing flight.

Then Twistmouth started gyrating
through the air."

"I started flying," Daddy says, "for the fun of it.
It was a dance derby, and I didn't even know it.
The cats were clapping, the floor was bouncing,
and my heart was beating.

And everybody was cheering, everybody..."

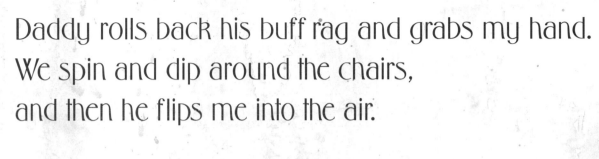

Daddy rolls back his buff rag and grabs my hand.
We spin and dip around the chairs,
and then he flips me into the air.

Daddy catches me and holds me close.
"Everybody," he says, "but your mama.
She was home counting out her own rhythms.
But somehow I heard her cries floating above the music,
and I fought my way through the crowds.

When you were born," my daddy says,
"I held you—so new you didn't even have a name yet—
high toward the heavens
so you could shine."

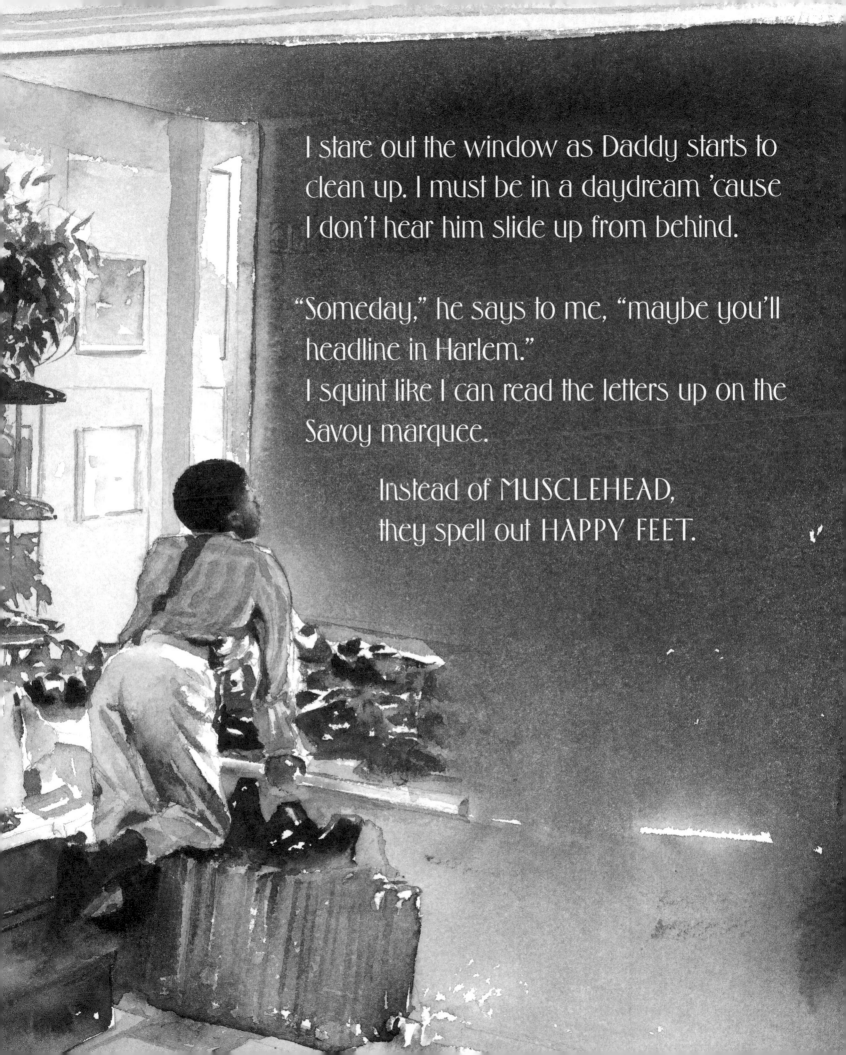

I stare out the window as Daddy starts to clean up. I must be in a daydream 'cause I don't hear him slide up from behind.

"Someday," he says to me, "maybe you'll headline in Harlem."
I squint like I can read the letters up on the Savoy marquee.

Instead of MUSCLEHEAD, they spell out HAPPY FEET.

Author's Notes

The Savoy Ballroom was Harlem's most famous dance club. It hosted celebrities, royalty, and most every big-name band and singer of the Swing Era (c. 1935–1940s), including Count Basie, Duke Ellington, and Ella Fitzgerald. The actress Lana Turner named the Savoy "the home of happy feet" because so many people went there to have a good time. The Savoy was one of the first ballrooms where black people and white people could dance together. It opened its doors in 1926 and closed in 1958.

The Lindy Hop was named after Charles Lindbergh's "hop," his historic first flight across the Atlantic Ocean in 1927. The dance, with its dizzy spins and joyful acrobatics, captured the excitement and optimism of the Harlem Renaissance. It reached its greatest popularity in 1937 when Whitey's Lindy Hoppers, starring Frankie "Musclehead" Manning, became a world-famous sensation, but the Lindy Hop remains one of America's most celebrated dances today.

Biographies

Leroy "Stretch" Jones stood six feet tall and was known for his grace on the dance floor. His friend and competitor "Shorty George" Snowden combined comic routines with groundbreaking energy and was known as the best of the early Savoy dancers.

Frankie "Musclehead" Manning, the Lindy Hop's reigning ambassador of goodwill, was born in 1914. He joined Whitey's Lindy Hoppers at age fifteen and took the Lindy to new heights of popularity by choreographing ecstatic dance-ensemble routines and taking his show on the road. Over the years he has appeared on television, on Broadway, and in numerous films.

Herbert "Whitey" White, nicknamed for his prominent streak of white hair, was a tough-talking ex-boxer and former bouncer at the Savoy. He trained and nurtured Whitey's Lindy Hoppers, the group of energetic young Harlem dancers who would forever change the dance style of America and the world by merging jazz rhythms and African beats with European melodies and ballroom-style structure.

"Long-Legged George" Grenidge created the Long-Legged Charleston, which exaggerated the length of his kicks by adding a forward and backward slide. "Twistmouth" George Ganaway invented the twist step (a swivel replacing the basic back step) for ladies. He also influenced Frankie Manning and discovered Norma Miller (one of Whitey's greatest Lindy Hoppers and a frequent partner of Frankie Manning) dancing on the street outside the Savoy when she was only fourteen years old.

Big Bea, six feet tall, and her less-than-five-feet-tall partner, Shorty George, were queen and king of the Savoy. Big Bea developed an over-the-back routine (she flipping him) that inspired Frankie Manning to develop his famous air step. Frankie tossed his partner into the air and caught her again, while both continued to dance in time to the music, making the Lindy Hop a real showstopper.